Wedding Planner

_____

&

_____

Wedding Contacts

● Wedding Planner

Name: ....

Email: ....

Web: ....

Phone: ....

Location: ....

....

● Reception Venue

Name: ....

Email: ....

Web: ....

Phone: ....

Location: ....

....

● Caterer

Name: ....

Email: ....

Web: ....

Phone: ....

Location: ....

....

● Ceremony Venue

Name: ....

Email: ....

Web: ....

Phone: ....

Location: ....

....

● Officiant

Name: ....

Email: ....

Web: ....

Phone: ....

Location: ....

....

● Photographer

Name: ....

Email: ....

Web: ....

Phone: ....

Location: ....

....

● Videographer

Name: ....

Email: ....

Web: ....

Phone: ....

Location: ....

....

● Florist

Name: ....

Email: ....

Web: ....

Phone: ....

Location: ....

Wedding Contacts

● Shop / Dress Designer

Name: ....

Email: ....

Web: ....

Phone: ....

Location: ....

....

● Bridal Shop

Name: ....

Email: ....

Web: ....

Phone: ....

Location: ....

....

● Bridal Jewelry

Name: ....

Email: ....

Web: ....

Phone: ....

Location: ....

....

● Hair Stylist

Name: ....

Email: ....

Web: ....

Phone: ....

Location: ....

....

● Makeup Artist

Name: ....

Email: ....

Web: ....

Phone: ....

Location: ....

....

● Stationery Designer

Name: ....

Email: ....

Web: ....

Phone: ....

Location: ....

....

● DJ Party Entertainment

Name: ....

Email: ....

Web: ....

Phone: ....

Location: ....

....

● Honeymoon Hotel/

Resort Name: ....

Email: ....

Web: ....

Phone: ....

Location: ....

Wedding Contacts

● Welcome Party Venue

Name: ....

Email: ....

Web: ....

Phone: ....

Location: ....

....

● Rehearsal Dinner Venue:

Name: ....

Email: ....

Web: ....

Phone: ....

Location: ....

....

● Wedding cake:

Name: ....

Email: ....

Web: ....

Phone: ....

Location: ....

....

● Other:

Name: ....

Email: ....

Web: ....

Phone: ....

Location: ....

....

●

Name: ....

Email: ....

Web: ....

Phone: ....

Location: ....

....

●

Name: ....

Email: ....

Web: ....

Phone: ....

Location: ....

....

●

Name: ....

Email: ....

Web: ....

Phone: ....

Location: ....

....

●

Name: ....

Email: ....

Web: ....

Phone: ....

Location: ....

....

# Important Dates

Notes

Date:	Date:	Date:

Date:	Date:	Date:

Date:	Date:	Date:

Date:	Date:	Date:

Date:	Date:	Date:

Important Dates

Date:

Date:

Date:

Notes

Date:

Date:

Date:

Date:

Date:

Date:

Date:

Date:

Date:

Date:

Date:

Date:

Wedding Budget

Details	Cost	Deposit	Remainder

Notes & Details

....
....
....
....
....
....

 # Wedding Budget

Details	Cost	Deposit	Remainder

Notes & Details

....
....
....
....
....
....

# Wedding Budget

Details	Cost	Deposit	Remainder

Notes & Details

....
....
....
....
....

 # Wedding Budget

Details	Cost	Deposit	Remainder

Notes & Details

....
....
....
....
....

Wedding Budget

Details	Cost	Deposit	Remainder

Notes & Details

....
....
....
....
....
....

Wedding Budget

Details	Cost	Deposit	Remainder

Notes & Details

....

....

....

....

....

Wedding Budget

Details	Cost	Deposit	Remainder

Notes & Details

....
....
....
....
....

 # Wedding Budget

Details	Cost	Deposit	Remainder

Notes & Details

....
....
....
....
....
....

 # Wedding Budget

Details	Cost	Deposit	Remainder

Notes & Details

....
....
....
....
....
....

Wedding Budget

Details	Cost	Deposit	Remainder

Notes & Details

....
....
....
....
....
....

Expense Snapshot
Ceremony Expense Tracker

Details	Budget	Cost	Deposit	Balance	Due Date
Officiant Gratuity					
Marriage License					
Venue Cost					
Flowers					
Decorations					

Notes & Details
....
....
....
....
....
....

Expense Snapshot
Reception Expense Tracker

Details	Budget	Cost	Deposit	Balance	Due Date
Venue Fee					
Catering					
Bar / Beverages					
Cake / Cutting Fee					
Decorations					
Rental					
Bartender Fee					

Notes & Details	
	....
....
....
....
....
....

Checklist
12 Months Before

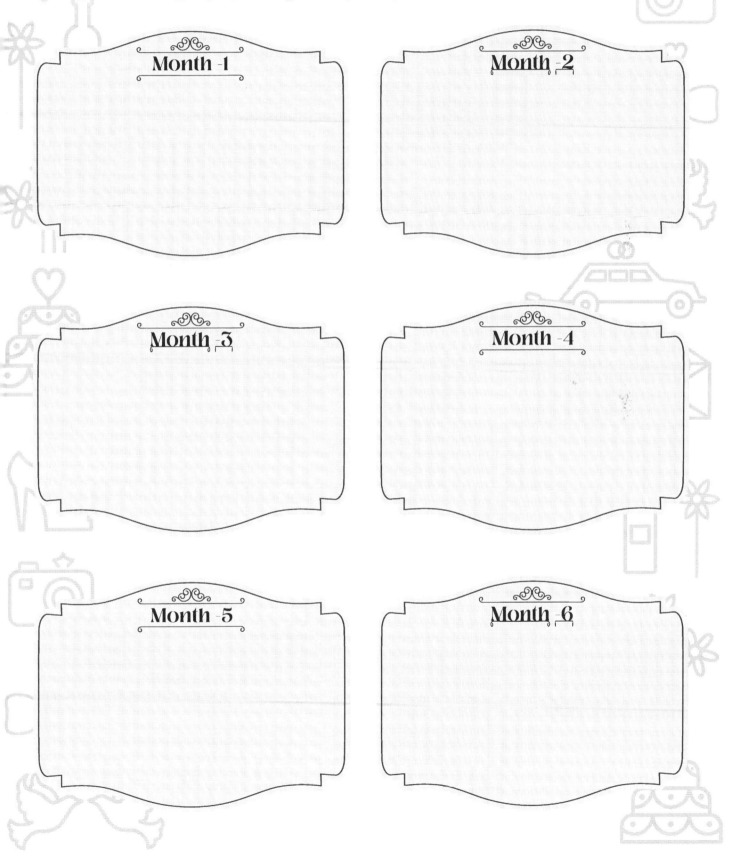

Month -1

Month -2

Month -3

Month -4

Month -5

Month -6

Checklist
12 Months Before

Month -7

Month -8

Month -9

Month -10

Month -11

Month -12

Guest List

Name	Phone	Email/Address

Guest List

Name	Phone	Email/Address

 # Guest List

Name	Phone	Email/Address

Guest List

Name	Phone	Email/Address

Guest List

Name	Phone	Email/Address

 # Guest List

Name	Phone	Email/Address

 # Guest List

Name	Phone	Email/Address
....	....	....
....	....	....
....	....	....
....	....	....
....	....	....
....	....	....
....	....	....
....	....	....
....	....	....
....	....	....
....	....	....
....	....	....
....	....	....
....	....	....
....	....	....
....	....	....
....	....	....
....	....	....
....	....	....

Guest List

Name	Phone	Email/Address

Guest List

Name	Phone	Email/Address

 # Guest List

Name	Phone	Email/Address

Guest List

Name	Phone	Email/Address

 # Guest List

Name	Phone	Email/Address

Guest List

Name	Phone	Email/Address

Guest List

Name	Phone	Email/Address

 # Guest List

Name	Phone	Email/Address

To Do List

- ☑ ....
- ☑ ....
- ☑ ....
- ☑ ....
- ☑ ....
- ☑ ....
- ☑ ....
- ☑ ....
- ☑ ....
- ☑ ....
- ☑ ....
- ☑ ....
- ☑ ....
- ☑ ....
- ☑ ....
- ☑ ....

- ☑ ....
- ☑ ....
- ☑ ....
- ☑ ....
- ☑ ....
- ☑ ....
- ☑ ....
- ☑ ....
- ☑ ....
- ☑ ....
- ☑ ....
- ☑ ....
- ☑ ....
- ☑ ....
- ☑ ....
- ☑ ....

Planning Notes

To Do List

- ♡ --
- ♡ --
- ♡ --
- ♡ --
- ♡ --
- ♡ --
- ♡ --
- ♡ --
- ♡ --
- ♡ --
- ♡ --
- ♡ --
- ♡ --
- ♡ --
- ♡ --
- ♡ --
- ♡ --

- ♡ --
- ♡ --
- ♡ --
- ♡ --
- ♡ --
- ♡ --
- ♡ --
- ♡ --
- ♡ --
- ♡ --
- ♡ --
- ♡ --
- ♡ --
- ♡ --
- ♡ --
- ♡ --
- ♡ --

Planning Notes

To Do List

Planning Notes

To Do List

Planning Notes

To Do List

- ....
- ....
- ....
- ....
- ....
- ....
- ....
- ....
- ....
- ....
- ....
- ....
- ....
- ....
- ....

- ....
- ....
- ....
- ....
- ....
- ....
- ....
- ....
- ....
- ....
- ....
- ....
- ....
- ....
- ....

Planning Notes

To Do List

Planning Notes

To Do List

Planning Notes

To Do List

Planning Notes

To Do List

- ....
- ....
- ....
- ....
- ....
- ....
- ....
- ....
- ....
- ....
- ....
- ....
- ....
- ....
- ....
- ....
- ....

- ....
- ....
- ....
- ....
- ....
- ....
- ....
- ....
- ....
- ....
- ....
- ....
- ....
- ....
- ....
- ....
- ....

Planning Notes

To Do List

Planning Notes

To Do List

Planning Notes

To Do List

Planning Notes

To Do List

- ♡ ....
- ♡ ....
- ♡ ....
- ♡ ....
- ♡ ....
- ♡ ....
- ♡ ....
- ♡ ....
- ♡ ....
- ♡ ....
- ♡ ....
- ♡ ....
- ♡ ....
- ♡ ....
- ♡ ....
- ♡ ....
- ♡ ....

- ♡ ....
- ♡ ....
- ♡ ....
- ♡ ....
- ♡ ....
- ♡ ....
- ♡ ....
- ♡ ....
- ♡ ....
- ♡ ....
- ♡ ....
- ♡ ....
- ♡ ....
- ♡ ....
- ♡ ....
- ♡ ....
- ♡ ....

Planning Notes

To Do List

Planning Notes

To Do List

Planning Notes

To Do List

- ....
- ....
- ....
- ....
- ....
- ....
- ....
- ....
- ....
- ....
- ....
- ....
- ....
- ....
- ....
- ....

- ....
- ....
- ....
- ....
- ....
- ....
- ....
- ....
- ....
- ....
- ....
- ....
- ....
- ....
- ....
- ....

Planning Notes

To Do List

Planning Notes

To Do List

Planning Notes

To Do List

Planning Notes

To Do List

Planning Notes

To Do List

Planning Notes

To Do List

Planning Notes

To Do List

Planning Notes

To Do List

Planning Notes

To Do List

Planning Notes

To Do List

Planning Notes

To Do List

Planning Notes

To Do List

To Do List

To Do List

Gift List

Date	Gift Description	Given by	Thank You Sent
			♡
			♡
			♡
			♡
			♡
			♡
			♡
			♡
			♡
			♡
			♡
			♡
			♡
			♡
			♡
			♡
			♡
			♡

Note & Details:

Gift List

Date	Gift Description	Given by	Thank You Sent
			♡
			♡
			♡
			♡
			♡
			♡
			♡
			♡
			♡
			♡
			♡
			♡
			♡
			♡
			♡
			♡
			♡
			♡
			♡

Note & Details:
....
....
....
....
....
....

Gift List

Date	Gift Description	Given by	Thank You Sent
			♡
			♡
			♡
			♡
			♡
			♡
			♡
			♡
			♡
			♡
			♡
			♡
			♡
			♡
			♡
			♡
			♡
			♡

Note & Details:

....
....
....
....
....
....

Gift List

Date	Gift Description	Given by	Thank You Sent
			♡
			♡
			♡
			♡
			♡
			♡
			♡
			♡
			♡
			♡
			♡
			♡
			♡
			♡
			♡
			♡
			♡

Note & Details:

Gift List

Date	Gift Description	Given by	Thank You Sent
			♡
			♡
			♡
			♡
			♡
			♡
			♡
			♡
			♡
			♡
			♡
			♡
			♡
			♡
			♡
			♡
			♡
			♡

Note & Details:

....
....
....
....
....

Gift List

Date	Gift Description	Given by	Thank You Sent
			♡
			♡
			♡
			♡
			♡
			♡
			♡
			♡
			♡
			♡
			♡
			♡
			♡
			♡
			♡
			♡
			♡
			♡

Note & Details: ....
....
....
....
....

Gift List

Date	Gift Description	Given by	Thank You Sent
			♡
			♡
			♡
			♡
			♡
			♡
			♡
			♡
			♡
			♡
			♡
			♡
			♡
			♡
			♡
			♡
			♡
			♡

Note & Details:
....
....
....
....
....

Gift List

Date	Gift Description	Given by	Thank You Sent
			♡
			♡
			♡
			♡
			♡
			♡
			♡
			♡
			♡
			♡
			♡
			♡
			♡
			♡
			♡
			♡
			♡
			♡

Note & Details: ....

....

....

....

....

Gift List

Date	Gift Description	Given by	Thank You Sent
			♡
			♡
			♡
			♡
			♡
			♡
			♡
			♡
			♡
			♡
			♡
			♡
			♡
			♡
			♡
			♡
			♡

Note & Details:
....
....
....
....
....
....

Gift List

Date	Gift Description	Given by	Thank You Sent
			♡
			♡
			♡
			♡
			♡
			♡
			♡
			♡
			♡
			♡
			♡
			♡
			♡
			♡
			♡
			♡
			♡
			♡

Note & Details: ....
....
....
....
....
....

Gift List

Date	Gift Description	Given by	Thank You Sent
			♡
			♡
			♡
			♡
			♡
			♡
			♡
			♡
			♡
			♡
			♡
			♡
			♡
			♡
			♡
			♡
			♡
			♡

Note & Details: ....
....
....
....
....
....

 # Gift List

Date	Gift Description	Given by	Thank You Sent
			♡
			♡
			♡
			♡
			♡
			♡
			♡
			♡
			♡
			♡
			♡
			♡
			♡
			♡
			♡
			♡
			♡
			♡
			♡

Note & Details: ....
....
....
....
....
....

Gift List

Date	Gift Description	Given by	Thank You Sent
			♡
			♡
			♡
			♡
			♡
			♡
			♡
			♡
			♡
			♡
			♡
			♡
			♡
			♡
			♡
			♡
			♡
			♡

Note & Details:

....

....

....

....

....

Gift List

Date	Gift Description	Given by	Thank You Sent
			♡
			♡
			♡
			♡
			♡
			♡
			♡
			♡
			♡
			♡
			♡
			♡
			♡
			♡
			♡
			♡
			♡
			♡

Note & Details: ....
....
....
....
....

 # Gift List

Date	Gift Description	Given by	Thank You Sent
			♡
			♡
			♡
			♡
			♡
			♡
			♡
			♡
			♡
			♡
			♡
			♡
			♡
			♡
			♡
			♡
			♡
			♡

Note & Details:
....
....
....
....
....
....

Gift List

Date	Gift Description	Given by	Thank You Sent
			♡
			♡
			♡
			♡
			♡
			♡
			♡
			♡
			♡
			♡
			♡
			♡
			♡
			♡
			♡
			♡
			♡
			♡

Note & Details: ....
....
....
....
....
....

Gift List

Date	Gift Description	Given by	Thank You Sent
			♡
			♡
			♡
			♡
			♡
			♡
			♡
			♡
			♡
			♡
			♡
			♡
			♡
			♡
			♡
			♡
			♡
			♡

Note & Details: ....
....
....
....
....
....

"A successful marriage
is an edifice that must be
rebuilt every day"

- Andre Maurois-

Made in the USA
Las Vegas, NV
03 January 2024